Inspiration and Meaning
Drawn From the Serenity of the Sea

By Dean Walley
Designed by David R. Miles

Hallmark Crown Editions

Printed in the United States of America.
Library of Congress Catalog Card Number: 73-78222.
Standard Book Number: 87529-347-6.

The seashore welcomes each visitor
with the promise of sunlit discovery,
and those who come to the sea to be refreshed and renewed
can share the blessings of serenity and return home again,
inspired and restored by the spirit of the sea.

Here we find the difference
between being alone...and loneliness.

Those who walk alone are never lonely...
...when they hear the voices of the sea
whispering along with the wind...
...and see the face of the sea
smiling back at the day
and dreaming in the moonlight...
...when they feel the hand of the sea
reaching out cool fingers
to comfort and caress.

The sea asks only that we lay down our burdens

on the smooth sand.

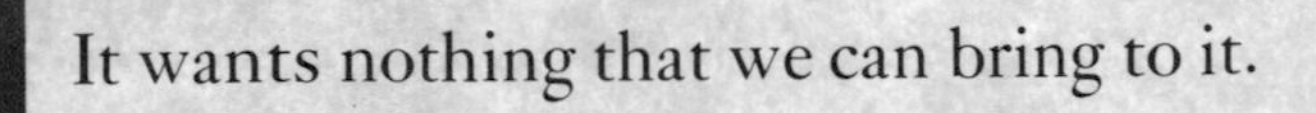

It wants nothing that we can bring to it.

All our treasures seem faded
beside its emerald majesty...

...and when all that encumbers us is cast into the

sea, we receive a greater treasure... peace of mind.

This outward simplification of life
...the freedom from possessions...
is only a beginning,
the first leg on a voyage into ourselves.

And as time ebbs away
curling moments into the fluid treasury of the sea...
we begin to give up our invisible burdens
of confusion...
...boredom...
...despair...
clearing a place within us
into which the ocean's peace and tranquillity can flow.

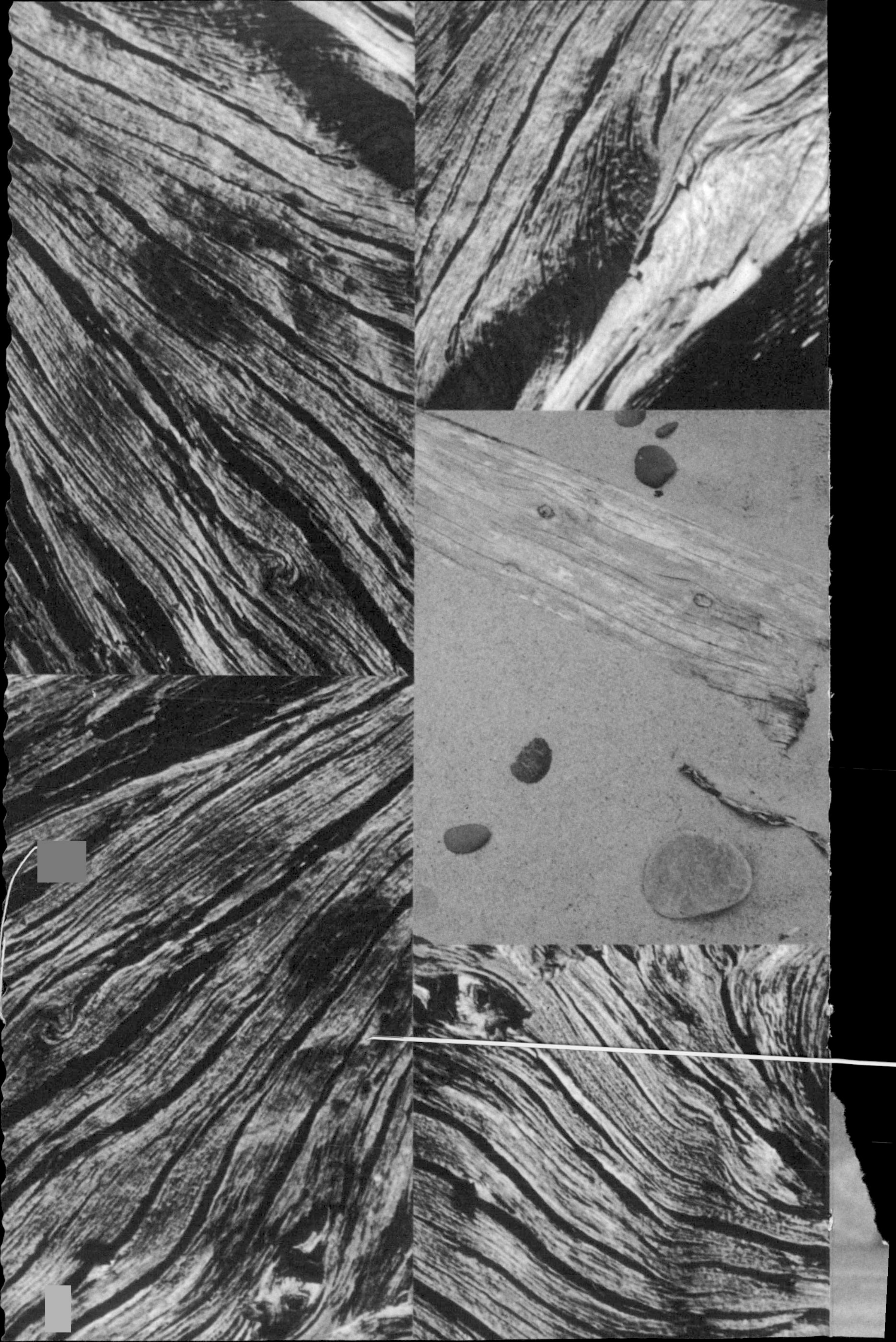

The rocky coast reminds us of the unyielding strength
of the human spirit... standing firm and proud
against the problems of life...
...even as the rocks
resist the onslaught
of the churning surf.

The ebb and flow of the sea is like the ebb and flow of friendship...

In the bleached and weathered beauty of driftwood...
...worn smooth by the waves and purified by the sun...
we see how time and hardship
can work to fashion all things in grace and dignity...

...even our own hearts.

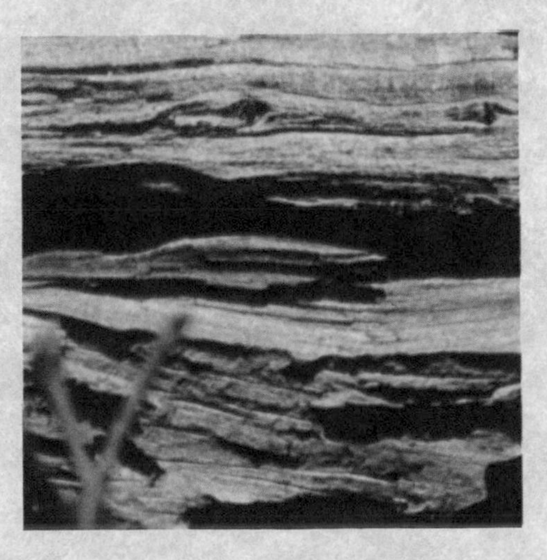

The ocean is a place of many patterns...
...gulls swirling overhead,
making white spirals on the blue sky...
...the white-edged filigree of the waves,
extending their pattern
to the limits of the horizon...
...and beyond...
...with schools of fish
coursing, wheeling, turning
through jade green depths.

love... and life.

Like the sea, all our relationships...
...our very existence...
wax and wane
depleting our levels of faith and hope,
then filling us again with a surge of joy...
...that lets us believe once more
in everything we love...
...and in ourselves.

The sea has cast up so many treasures for us.
The beach is dotted with shells of every description...
...furled and latticed by nature's artistry...sculptured and turned...

bleached to a dazzling white or shimmering with a pearly sheen.

At first we want them all...

we run to catch each one...

...but soon we realize

that these are only shells...

empty houses left by the creatures of the sea...

...and we lay all but the most beautiful aside

and carry one or two away with us.

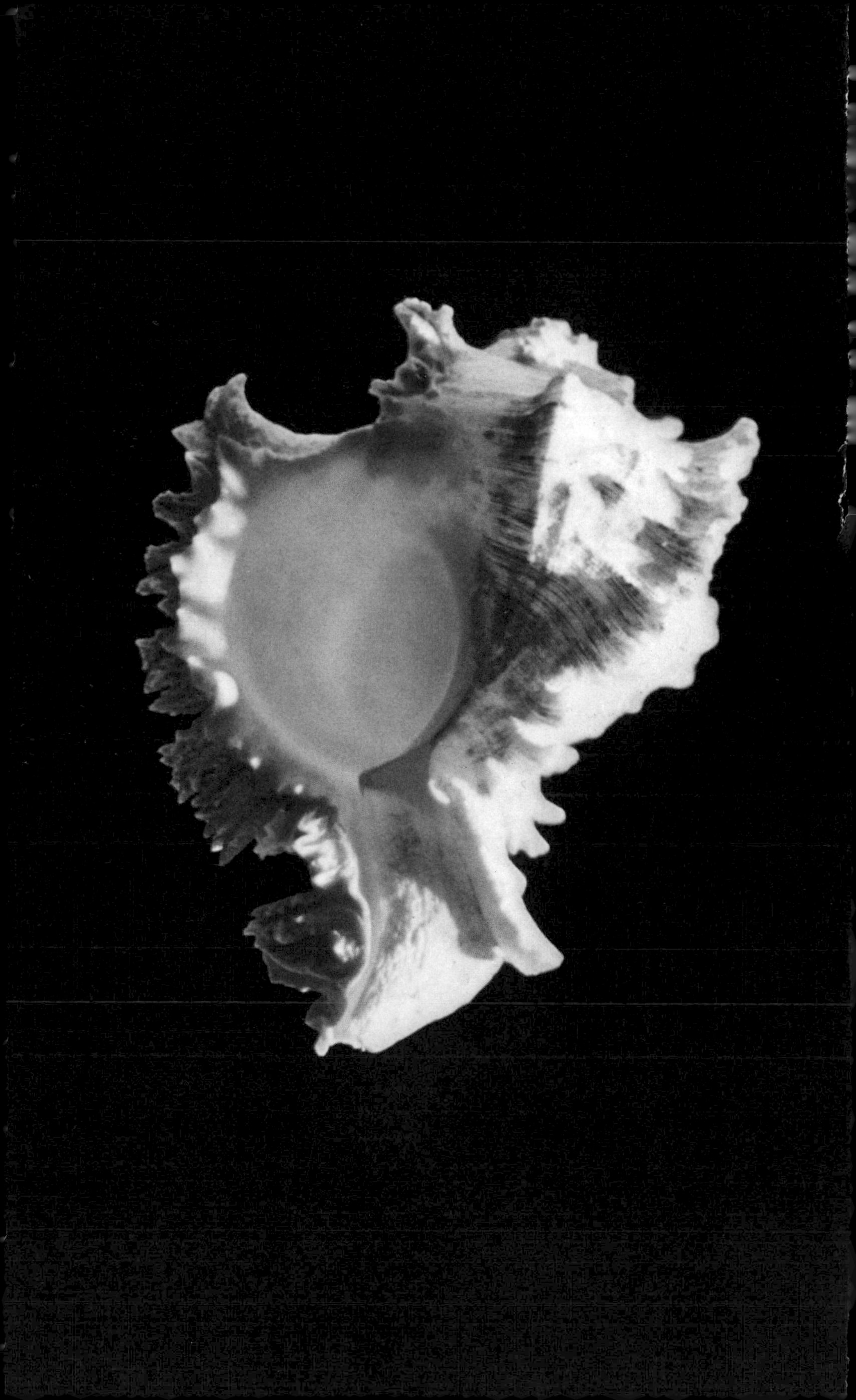

Just as one cannot collect all the beautiful shells on the beach,
so one cannot collect all the moments of wonder...
...all the songs of joy...
...all the times of triumph that are a part of life.

But we can clasp the ones that come to us...
...close to our hearts...
where they will remain forever.

In listening to the sea...
in peering into its vastness...
we learn many lessons...

...the patience that reduces mountains
to tiny grains of sand...
...the faith that allows the tides to flow away...
...freeing them from the bonds of earth...
knowing they will return again and again...

...and we learn of the simplicity of nature
that strips away the complexity of civilization
and helps us...
...through solitude...
to grow close to the Power of Creation.

And when we leave the sea
...as it cradles the sun with its arms...
we will walk the steps to home
...with a perfect peace...
...with a quiet joy...

...with a full heart.

The illustrations in this book
are executed in photomontage,
a creative technique in which
separate photos are combined
by the designer to produce
a composite picture.
The typeface is Janson,
created by Nicholas Kis in
Amsterdam around 1690.
The cover is bound with
book cloth and Torino paper.
Inside pages are Hallclear
and White Imitation Parchment.
Book design by David R. Miles.